Texas Myths and Legends
Stories of the Frontier

This book was developed in conjunction with a statewide traveling public art project produced by the Center for Contemporary Arts in Abilene, Texas. The pictures in this book are from the Texas Myths and Legends exhibit.

TEXAS MYTHS AND LEGENDS
STORIES OF THE FRONTIER

John C. Ferguson

McWhiney Foundation Press
McMurry University
Abilene, Texas

Library of Congress Cataloging-in-Publication Data

Ferguson, John C. (John Craig), 1959-
    Texas myths & legends: stories of the frontier / John C. Ferguson.
    p. cm.
Includes bibliographical references.
    ISBN 1-893114-42-2 (pbk.)
1. Folklore—Texas. 2. Frontier and pioneer life—Texas—History. 3. Texas—Social life
and customs. I. Title: Texas myths and legends. II. Title.
    GR110.T5F47 2003
    398.2'09764—dc21

2003014395

Printed in the United States of America

ISBN 1-893114-42-2

10 9 8 7 6 5 4 3 2 1

Book Designed by Rosenbohm Graphic Design

The McWhiney Foundation Press is a nonprofit operation
devoted to the promotion of history education.
For telephone inquiries, call (325) 793-4682.

CONTENTS

Texas Myths and Legends
Stories of the Frontier

INTRODUCTION

America has long been a country of frontiers—and of people who have conquered frontiers. We are a nation of immigrants, people who were not content to stay where they were, but who wanted to see what was "over there." We are a nation of risk-takers, people who were willing to take a chance on the unknown.

Texas, something of a country within a country, was settled in the nineteenth century by the hardiest and most courageous of folks descended from pioneer stock. The Texas frontier was a vast, unsettled area which beckoned to the daring, an area that offered a fresh start. Those who had suffered financial misfortune or had brushes with the law could come out West and begin anew, if they had sufficient courage.

The frontier, or the line separating civilization from wilderness, was a fluid line, moving ever westward. The stories offered in this volume concern the inhabitants of the Texas frontier during a specific period in time, principally the last half of the nineteenth century into the early twentieth. The Texas frontier from the 1860s to the 1890s was roughly the area west of a line drawn from Fort Worth to San Antonio. During the 1860s and 1870s, Comanche and Kiowa Indians still ruled much of the area, and only the strong and the brave ventured into the region; the weak died along the way, and the timid never left home.

The frontier experience, of course, shaped the lives of the people who settled the area. The struggle against the elements, contending with primitive and harsh living conditions, struggling to take the land from an antagonistic foe, all made indelible impressions on the minds and beliefs and outlooks of early Texans.

The history of Texas is a grand and glorious story, a tale of heroes and villains, and some people who were both. We Texans have great pride in our state and in the accomplishments of those who came before us, but we have been known to brag, to exaggerate, to stretch a yarn, to embellish stories of our past. Over the course of time, some of the early inhabitants of our state may have become unrecognizable, larger than life, entered into the realm of myth or legend. The purpose of this collection is to cut through the romance and the fiction and to help explain—simply, succinctly, and objectively—some of the people who made Texas what it is today.

Here, then, are their stories.

THE COMANCHE

When a nomadic band of Indians migrated south and east from the Rocky Mountains in the late seventeenth century, they collided and fought with other Indian tribes. The Utes referred to these roaming Indians as "koh-mats," or "ones who want to fight me all the time." The early Spanish recorded the name as "komantcia," which the Anglos called Comanche. The Comanche referred to themselves simply as "The People."

Leaving the mountains and moving onto the plains, the Comanche acquired horses by either stealing them from other Indian tribes or the Spaniards, or by capturing wild mustangs running free on the abundant grasslands of western and central North America. The Comanche people adapted well to the mounted life and incorporated horses into their hunting and warfare. Swift-moving raiders, the Comanche ranged across present Oklahoma, New Mexico, Texas, and deep into Mexico seeking, and acquiring, horses and plunder, while terrorizing the Spanish settlers and their Mexican successors.

Early Anglo-American settlers in Texas initially had more peaceful relations with the Comanche, a relationship fostered and encouraged by Stephen F. Austin, leader of the American immigrants in Texas. These Anglo-American newcomers settled along the rich river bottoms of southeast Texas, far from Comanche hunting grounds. But soon the whites began moving farther north and west, invading traditional Comanche lands.

Brothers James and Silas Parker, along with several other frontier families, built a small settlement on the Navasota River in present Limestone County, east of Waco. On the morning of May 19, 1836, several hundred mounted Comanche and Kiowa warriors attacked Parker's Fort, killing several inhabitants and riding off with five captives. One of the victims, nine-year-old Cynthia Ann Parker, lived with the Indians for twenty-four years, and became the wife of one Comanche chief and the mother of another. This was only the first of many instances in which the Comanche seized Anglo women and children, actions that provoked great hatred among the whites toward the Indians.

In the years that followed, relations between the Texans and the Comanche alternated between periods of uneasy, distrustful peace and open warfare. Both sides signed and then violated peace treaties, but the white settlers steadily encroached further and further into lands considered sacrosanct by the Comanche. The final telling blow came with the obliteration of the great buffalo herds.

The American bison, popularly known as the buffalo, was the source of food and shelter to the Indians of the plains tribes. Indians made clothing and tepees from the hides, tools and utensils from the horns and bones, and ate the meat of the shaggy beasts. White settlers also killed the buffalo for their meat, but when eastern tanners devised a way to make leather from the thick buffalo skins, they created a new market. Buffalo hunters made enormous sums of money selling the hides, and in the 1870s thousands of hunters swarmed over the plains from Kansas to Texas decimating the herds.

The Comanche and other plains Indians realized that the buffalo hunters were exterminating their source of food and sustenance, and in 1874 they made a concerted effort to rid the plains of the white hunters. On June 27, 1874, several hundred Comanche, Kiowa, and Cheyenne warriors under the leadership of Quanah Parker and Isa-tai attacked the trading center of Adobe Walls, in present Hutchinson County. Isa-tai, a Comanche medicine man, convinced the Indians that the bullets of the white

Quanah Parker

When Comanche raiders kidnapped young Cynthia Ann Parker in 1836, no one could have predicted that her son would one day become the last great war chief of the Comanche Indians. As Cynthia Ann grew older, the Comanche Chieftain Peta Nocona took her to be his wife, and in about 1845 she gave birth to their first child, a boy named Quanah.

Quanah Parker, half Texan and half Comanche, became a war leader during the mid 1870s, a time during which the United States Army and the Texas Rangers constantly pursued the Comanche in Texas. More importantly, hunters were rapidly exterminating the buffalo, the source of sustenance of the Comanche. The Army, led by the redoubtable Colonel Ranald S. Mackenzie, constantly pursued Quanah Parker but never defeated him in battle. Buffalo hunters on the Texas plains accomplished what the Army could not. The lack of a food source, along with the constant harassment of the Army, finally forced Quanah and his followers to seek refuge in the Kiowa-Comanche reservation in southwestern Indian Territory, now the state of Oklahoma.

Unlike most Indians, Quanah quickly adopted the white man's ways and made a successful transition to the reservation life. He was obviously a man of superior intelligence, and the agent in charge of the reservation named him chief of all the Comanche Indians, a decision the leaderless tribe accepted.

In his position of leadership Quanah encouraged education of the Indian youth and constructed schools on the reservation. Quanah also leased Comanche grazing lands to white ranchers and supported Comanche farming and business ventures. As the last great Comanche chief, Quanah Parker helped his people bridge the gap between the Comanche world of their past and the white world of their future.

men could not harm them. He was wrong. The buffalo hunters, with powerful rifles and abundant ammunition, killed many of the attacking Indians and forced the others to pull back out of range of the buffalo guns. After a half-hearted siege, the attacking Indians withdrew on July 1.

The Battle at Adobe Walls was an Indian disaster in that they killed only three buffalo hunters while scores of Indians were killed or wounded. More importantly, the battle precipitated the Army's campaign to round up the hostile Indians. During the Red River War of 1874-75 Colonel Ranald Mackenzie commanded Army troops that captured and destroyed the stores, shelters, clothing and horses of the combative Cheyenne, Comanche, and Kiowa Indians. Although the soldiers killed but a few Indians, the remainder were left dismounted, hungry, and without supplies. Defeated and disheartened, the various bands of hostiles eventually surrendered and submitted to reservation life. The once feared Comanche Indian had entered the realm of history.

SUGGESTED READINGS

Clayton, Lawrence and Joan Halford Farmer, eds. *Tracks Along the Clear Fork.* Abilene: McWhiney Foundation Press, 2000.

Fehrenbach, T.R. *Comanches: The Destruction of a People.* New York: Alfred A. Knopf, 1974.

Neely, Bill. *The Last Comanche Chief: The Life and Times of Quanah Parker.* New York: John Wiley and Sons, 1995.

Rister, Carl Coke. *Border Captives.* Norman: University of Oklahoma Press, 1940.

Richardson, Rupert Norval. *The Comanche Barrier to South Plains Settlement.* Glendale, California: The Arthur H. Clark Company, 1933.

Wallace, Ernest and E. Adamson Hoebel. *The Comanches: Lords of the South Plains.* Norman: University of Oklahoma Press, 1952.

THE BUFFALO SOLDIER

Black Americans have served our country, and in the armed forces of our country, since the American Revolution. Crispus Attucks was among the first Americans to give their lives life for liberty in 1770. Black soldiers fought the British at the Battle of Bunker Hill, served with General Washington when he crossed the Delaware, and fought with distinction under General Andrew Jackson at the Battle of New Orleans in 1815.

During the American Civil War of 1861 to 1865 entire regiments of black soldiers served in the Union Army. By the end of that fratricidal conflict, almost 180,000 blacks had worn the uniform of their country. More than 33,000 gave their lives for ideals like freedom, justice, and union. But until 1866 the United States Army did not recruit blacks during peacetime. That practice soon changed.

Setting forth the size and structure of the peacetime Army, Congress recognized the valiant service of blacks by authorizing two regiments each of black infantry and cavalry. The four black regiments were the Twenty-fourth and Twenty-fifth Infantry Regiments, and the Ninth and Tenth Cavalry Regiments. After 1869 black soldiers composed ten per cent of the United States Army and twenty per cent of the cavalry.

When at full strength, infantry regiments of the time consisted of ten companies of fifty men each. Cavalry regiments contained twelve companies, later called troops, of seventy men. While intelligent and responsible soldiers could expect promotion to corporal or sergeant, almost all commissioned officers of the black regiments were white. One notable exception was Lieutenant Henry Flipper, the first black to graduate from West Point, in 1877.

Many of the men who became soldiers in the black regiments had served in the Union Army during the Civil War. Other recruits were freed slaves from the Southern states and free blacks from the border states as well as the North. Once they became soldiers, the men did much more than simply carry a rifle or ride a cavalry horse. Black soldiers became cooks, clerks, bakers, blacksmiths, farriers, and saddlers. Other essential members of Army regiments of the time included musicians, printers, telegraphers, and tailors.

After the admission of Texas into the union prior to the Civil War, both the Texas Rangers and the United States Army patrolled the Texas frontier, protecting settlers from the depredations of hostile Indians and marauding outlaw bands from Mexico. One of the most notable Army units that had this duty was the famed Second Cavalry Regiment. Officers who served in this regiment included Robert E. Lee, Albert Sidney Johnston, and others who achieved prominence during the Civil War.

After the Civil War, beginning in 1867, black soldiers protected the Southern border of the United States and scouted along the Western frontier, the limit of civilized settlements. Their duties consisted of patrolling the vast expanses of the West, as well as building and maintaining frontier posts such as Fort McKavett, Fort Concho, Fort Griffin, and others.

The Comanche Indians first conferred the name "Buffalo Soldiers" on the black cavalry troopers at Fort Sill in 1873, in reference to the curly black hair of the soldiers. The name stuck, and by 1890 newspapers throughout the country widely referred to all black soldiers as Buffalo Soldiers. The name became a symbol of pride for black soldiers.

The pay of black and white soldiers was the same, thirteen dollars a month after 1878, and the Army was one of the few occupations that offered equal compensa-

Emanuel Stance

When Emanuel Stance entered the recruiter's office in Lake Providence, Louisiana, in October 1866, he favorably impressed the recruiting officer. Although just over five feet tall, the nineteen-year-old sharecropper could read and write, an exceptional ability for black men of that time. Just ten months after his enlistment, the Army promoted Stance to sergeant because of his intelligence and ability to handle paperwork. But Sergeant Emanuel Stance was no mere paper-shuffler: he was a courageous fighter.

Assigned to Company F, Ninth United States Cavalry, Sergeant Stance soon went west to protect the Texas frontier from marauding Indians. While stationed at Fort McKavett, Sergeant Stance led a patrol of ten troopers to seek out and punish Kickapoo Indians that had raided nearby settlements and captured two white children.

On May 19, 1870, Stance led his patrol in an attack on a group of Indians driving a herd of stolen horses. The Indians scattered, and the Buffalo Soldiers recovered the horses. The following day Stance discovered a band of Indians preparing to attack two government wagons, and he once again charged the enemy. Later in the day the Indians attacked the Army patrol, and Stance and his men repulsed the attack, recovering six more stolen horses. The Indians once more attacked Stance and his troopers as they were watering their weary horses, and the Buffalo Soldiers again routed the hostiles.

Sergeant Stance continued with his patrol, eventually recovering the two kidnapped children and returning them to safety. For his exceptional gallantry in combat, the President of the United States awarded the Medal of Honor to Sergeant Emanuel Stance on June 28, 1870.

tion for blacks. While a soldier's life was often rugged and austere, it did offer a measure of security, a home, and regular meals, even if they only consisted of bread, beans, beef, and coffee. During the last three decades of the nineteenth century, the black regulars had a lower rate of desertion and a higher rate of reenlistment than white regiments. This may have been a result of fewer economic opportunities for blacks in the civilian world as well as the relative equality and respect afforded black men in the army.

Black soldiers protected the Texas frontier from 1867 to 1885. Men in the black regiments served with honor and distinction, often fighting racial prejudice as well as hostile Indians. Over time, the soldiers of the black regiments, and the service they performed, came to be widely respected and appreciated by the people of Texas.

SUGGESTED READINGS

Carroll, John M., ed. *The Black Military Experience in the American West*. New York: Liveright, 1971.

Clayton, Lawrence and Joan Halford Farmer, eds. *Tracks Along the Clear Fork*. Abilene: McWhiney Foundation Press, 2000.

Dobak, William A. and Thomas D. Phillips. *The Black Regulars: 1866-1898*. Norman: University of Oklahoma Press, 2001.

Leckie, William H. *The Buffalo Soldiers*. Norman: University of Oklahoma Press, 1967.

Nalty, Bernard C. *Strength for the Fight: A History of Black Americans in the Military*. New York: Free Press, 1986.

Utley, Robert M. *Frontier Regulars: The United States Army and the Indian, 1866-1891*. New York: Macmillan, 1973.

THE BUFFALO HUNTER

The American bison, commonly known as the buffalo, was once the most abundant large animal in North America. In the 1850s biologists numbered the herds not by numbers of animals, but by the square miles they occupied. A solid herd of buffalo, five miles by twelve miles, was not uncommon. The vast grass-covered heart of North America, from the Rocky Mountains in the West to the Appalachian Mountains in the East, supported between thirty and sixty million buffalo in the early to mid nineteenth century. Massive animals, with short, upturned horns, buffalo have a thick hide and a full, dark-brown mat of heavy fur, and can weigh as much as 2,500 pounds.

The American Plains Indians relied on the buffalo as their primary source of sustenance. The shaggy brown animals provided an abundant supply of meat for food, hides and robes for clothing and shelter, and buffalo chips to burn for fuel. Indians even made tools and eating utensils from the bones and horns of the animals. In short, the Plains Indian culture was dependent upon the buffalo.

Early white settlers in the West also killed buffalo for meat and occasionally tanned the furry hides to make warm, though cumbersome, buffalo robes. The numbers of buffalo killed by Indians and pioneers for food and robes was inconsequential considering the vast numbers of the animals roaming the American plains. But by 1871 European and American tanneries had developed methods of making usable leather from dried buffalo hides, creating an overnight, and insatiable, demand for those hides.

The need for infinite numbers of buffalo skins created a new and terribly efficient industry of killing the shaggy beasts. Armed with powerful rifles, buffalo hunters by the thousands swarmed over the plains in pursuit of their prey. A hunting party generally consisted of four to a dozen men, with one or two men doing the shooting and the others doing the cooking, skinning, hide-handling, taking care of the wagons and teams, reloading ammunition, and keeping an eye out for Indians.

The hunters, also known as runners or hidemen, set out early in the morning to locate a herd of buffalo, approaching as near as possible without alarming the herd. Then the hunters began shooting the animals, trying to kill the ones on the fringes of the herd or any that began to walk away. It was important to kill them instantly and not allow a wounded buffalo to run about frightening the herd, causing it to stampede. Buffalo are not naturally skittish animals, and it was often possible for one or two shooters to kill more than a hundred buffalo at one location, or "stand."

After killing as many animals as could be processed in a day, the work of skinning the dead buffalo began. The hidemen then dried the skins in the sun and transported them to the nearest shipping point, where they sold the hides. From that point, the hide dealers sent the dried or "flint" hides to tanneries in the east, where they were made into leather or luxurious buffalo robes.

A number of Texas frontier towns supported the buffalo hunting industry. In Rath City, Adobe Walls, or Fort Griffin, hunters could sell their hides and buy essential supplies. The frontier depots also provided diversions for the hunting crews, as gamblers, saloonkeepers, and women of attainable virtue happily relieved the men of their earnings.

During the most prolific hunting years in Texas, 1874 to 1878, buffalo runners

Josiah Wright Mooar

Like many another restive young man of the time, J. Wright Mooar looked for adventure and excitement in the American West. In the fall of 1870, when he was just nineteen years old, young Wright left his native Vermont and found work as a woodchopper at Fort Hays, Kansas. Soldiers at the fort told the young man tales of vast numbers of buffalo on the plains, herds so immense they stretched from horizon to horizon. Mooar soon grew bored with cutting wood and decided to see the buffalo for himself.

Moving west to Dodge City, Mooar hunted buffalo to provide meat for the railroad crews then laying track across Kansas. It seemed wasteful to him to take only the meat, leaving the heavy fur-covered buffalo hide on the prairie to rot, so he sent some of the hides to his brother John, living in New York City, to see if he could find an Eastern market for the hides. John Mooar found that he could sell the hides to tanners for $3.50 each, to be tanned with the fur on and used for robes. The tanners placed an order for two thousand more skins, and the buffalo hide industry began in earnest.

Over the next several years J. Wright Mooar, sometimes with his brother and sometimes with other hunters, harvested thousands of the brown furry hides. Initially limiting their hunting activities to Kansas, in 1873 Mooar and other hunters moved their operations to the Texas panhandle. During these years on the plains Wright had several brushes with hostile Indians and narrowly escaped death at the hands of the harsh Texas winters.

During the brief years of the great slaughter, Mooar killed an estimated twenty thousand animals. After the destruction of the buffalo herds in Texas, he settled near Snyder in West Texas and conducted freighting and ranching operations in Scurry and Mitchell counties. One of the most prolific of the buffalo hunters, and then a successful rancher, J. Wright Mooar was an honored and respected West Texas pioneer.

shipped hundreds of thousands of hides out of Texas. During the 1876-77 season, for instance, hide dealers in Fort Griffin shipped over two hundred thousand hides. Within just a few seasons the hunters efficiently put themselves out of business. By 1879 the herds in Texas were wiped out, and by 1889 less than a hundred free-ranging buffalo remained in the United States. Ultimately it was not hunters that destroyed the buffalo, but the inexorable drive of American enterprise and the American consumer in the genteel and settled East. The hunters were simply supplying the demand.

While pursuing their own economic gain through the slaughter of the vast herds of buffalo, the hunters inadvertently made significant contributions to the final settlement of the Texas frontier. Elimination of the herds meant that large-scale cattle ranching could be introduced, and smaller ranchers and farmers could erect fences without migratory buffalo herds tearing them down. And by killing off the food source of the hostile Indians, the buffalo hunters helped drive the Indians onto the reservations, making the Texas frontier far safer for permanent settlement.

Suggested Readings

Anderson, Charles. *In Search of the Buffalo: The Story of J. Wright Mooar.* Seagraves, Texas: Pioneer Press, 1974.

Clayton, Lawrence and Joan Halford Farmer, eds. *Tracks Along the Clear Fork.* Abilene: McWhiney Foundation Press, 2000.

McHugh, Tom. *The Time of the Buffalo.* Lincoln: University of Nebraska Press, 1972.

Gard, Wayne. *The Great Buffalo Hunt.* New York: Knopf, 1960.

Robinson, Charles M. III. *The Buffalo Hunters.* Austin: State House Press, 1995.

THE SALOON GAL

One of the more important fixtures in the frontier community was the local drinking establishment. In addition to being a place where a man could quench his thirst, a saloon was also a club and a gathering place for men, where they could commiserate on the low prices of cattle or buffalo hides, the lack of rain, or the possibility of an Indian attack.

Many saloons offered more than alcoholic beverages, often serving as restaurants, grocery stores, post offices, and hotels. Some whiskey mills even doubled as courthouses, as evidenced by a saloon called the Jersey Lilly, the concern of Judge Roy Bean, "Law West of the Pecos," in Langtry, Texas. Saloons routinely outnumbered churches and often exceeded the number of all other businesses in frontier towns.

The first drinking establishments on the Texas frontier often consisted of a man with a barrel of whiskey peddling drinks out of the back of a wagon alongside the trail. Then he might upgrade to a board laid across two empty whiskey barrels serving as a bar, perhaps under a tent fly. Before long, he had made enough money from drifting cowhands, buffalo hunters, and day laborers that he could further improve his business. Then he would put up a wooden frame building with a long counter against one wall serving as a bar, complete with a brass rail upon which a thirsty individual could rest his foot. In those towns that appeared to be permanent, the owner of the establishment might bring in an elaborate, hand-carved, imported hardwood bar. A mahogany bar and a gilded mirror were signs of affluence, indeed.

A form of early democracy prevailed among the clientele in most frontier watering holes. Ranch owners might rub elbows with railroad section hands or well-dressed professional gamblers. Cowboys, either from nearby ranches or pushing a herd of steers up the trail, would be leaning on the bar next to buffalo hunters or local merchants. Nesters or small farmers, soldiers, and village tradesmen could all be found hoisting a glass together. The only group excluded from the friendly atmosphere of a saloon was women, unless they happened to work in the establishment.

Aside from the paying customers, three types of people regularly conducted business within frontier saloons. These were bartenders, gamblers, and saloon girls. Barkeepers, of course, were essential as dispensers of refreshment and the takers of payment, but very often they were much more than drink merchants. Early whiskey peddlers often were highly respected pillars of the community, serving as mayors, town councilmen or in other respected positions within the community. While some bartenders could be stern and hard-bitten when breaking up a fight, they more often were peacemakers and problem solvers.

Gamblers were another ubiquitous feature of the frontier watering hole. When the railroaders came to town after payday, or cowhands from a nearby spread decided it was time to cut the trail dust out of their throats, gamblers awaited them in the watering holes to separate the workingmen from their money. Card games such as poker or faro were most common, although some establishments with pretensions to class sported roulette wheels.

Perhaps the most interesting of the denizens of Texas whiskey mills were the saloon girls. Some women in such establishments were dancers, others lady gamblers, some hustled drinks from lonely men, and others sold their company. Prostitution

Lottie Deno

The West Texas community of San Angelo, across the river from Fort Concho, boasted many saloons and gambling establishments, as did most of the little towns that sprang up near frontier army posts. There was the usual rag-tag assortment of cardsharps, gamblers, and various leeches to take money from the soldiers, cowboys, and buffalo hunters that frequented the area.

Then one day in about 1870 a young lady stepped down off the stagecoach from San Antonio. This attractive woman with lush dark hair and sparkling black eyes dressed and comported herself as a refined, well-bred gentlewoman, yet she had one trait uncharacteristic of most society ladies: she was a gambler.

Going by the name of Mystic Maude, the newcomer to the town was certainly a mystery to those who knew her. She soon established herself as a regular among the gambling fraternity, playing high-stakes poker and winning far more often than losing. But she did not socialize with gamblers or anyone else away from the gambling tables. She lived alone in a little adobe building and refused to see any visitors, male or female.

Rumors about her background abounded, and an officer at Fort Concho circulated one particular tale. He related that the woman's father had been a Southern gentleman, and gambler, who died in the service of the Confederate Army. Since his death the young lady had supported her mother and sister the only way she knew how, by gambling.

Just as suddenly as she had appeared, the gambling lady disappeared from San Angelo, only to reappear at "the Flat," a parasite community down the hill from Fort Griffin, where she introduced herself as Lottie Deno. She soon reestablished herself as a master gambler, matching wits, and cards, with such frontier toughs as Wyatt Earp, "Doc" Holliday, and John Selman.

In 1877 Lottie Deno boarded a westbound stage and left Fort Griffin and Texas forever. Settling in New Mexico, the card queen married, quit gambling, and became a community benefactor. She didn't completely fade into obscurity, however. Television revived her memory when Miss Kitty portrayed her character in the long-running series "Gunsmoke."

was a common occurrence on the Texas frontier, and such businesses generally operated out of saloons. Most of the women who worked in the saloons were in their early twenties, with very few over the age of thirty. Women sold their wares in order to become economically independent or to escape an uneventful existence on a lonely farm or ranch. Some entered the sporting life for excitement, but most hoped to find a respectable man and settle down after making money. A few achieved their dreams of security and respectability, but many others ended their own lives with opium or other poisons or died of disease or alcoholism.

Saloons began to decline in prominence and popularity in Texas by the end of the nineteenth century as a result of the steadying influences of women and religion and the growing temperance movement. Shortly after the turn of the twentieth century some saloons in Texas were replaced by more genteel private clubs, but most simply faded into the past, along with the Texas frontier.

SUGGESTED READINGS

Erdoes, Richard. *Saloons of the Old West*. New York: Alfred A. Knopf, 1979.

Gard, Wayne. *Rawhide Texas*. Norman: University of Oklahoma Press, 1965.

Haney, Hood L. *Pioneer Living in Texas*. New York: Vantage Press, 1970.

Rosa, Joseph G. and Waldo E. Koop. *Rowdy Joe Lowe: Gambler With a Gun*. Norman: University of Oklahoma Press, 1989

Rose, Cynthia. *Lottie Deno: Gambling Queen of Hearts*. Santa Fe: Clear Light, 1994.

THE RANCHER

The history of Texas and the history of cattle ranching are so intertwined that they are almost inseparable. The importance of ranching as a Texas tradition and as a part of our heritage is difficult to overstate. Livestock formed the basis of the agricultural industry on the Texas frontier and became an essential component of the early Texas economy. Texas and ranching simply grew up together, as expressed by Albany resident Berta Nance: "Other states were carved or born, Texas grew from hide and horn."

Ranching in Texas began in the late seventeenth century when Spanish priests drove herds from Mexico to the new missions north of the Rio Grande. As Indian attacks caused the Spaniards to abandon many of their missions, they also abandoned their cattle. These cattle intermixed with English cattle the Anglo colonists brought into Texas, and the result was a large, rangy cow with massive horns. These crossbred wild cattle became the foundation of the vast herds of longhorns that populated the state and were the basis of the cattle industry in Texas.

The first Anglo colonists who came to Texas were farmers, not ranchers. But many of the early settlers saw opportunity in the lush grasslands of southeast Texas and the large numbers of wild cattle running free. Stock raising soon became a major business enterprise in the sparsely settled region.

One of the first significant ranchers in Texas was a riverboat operator named Richard King, who began buying large sections of South Texas land in 1852. A daring and discerning businessman, Richard King built his South Texas ranch into a cattle empire, covering hundreds of square miles of land. Beginning his ranching venture with longhorns, King soon imported purebred bulls to improve his herds. Eventually, the King Ranch became the most famous ranch in Texas, and King introduced such innovations as fencing of pastures and scientific breeding of livestock. When King died in 1885 he was among the richest men in Texas.

During the first years of the long and bloody Civil War, Texas ranchers supplied much of the beef for the Confederate Army. After the fall of Vicksburg in July 1863, however, Texans could no longer ship their cattle east across the Union-controlled Mississippi River. With no outlet for the cattle, their value declined. Also during this time, many stock raisers on the frontier abandoned their land and herds. Most of the able bodied men served in the Confederate Army, and many of those who remained retreated from the frontier toward the more settled East in the face of increased Indian activity. Neglected, the cattle became wild and grew in number.

When the war ended and ex-Confederate soldiers returned to their homes, millions of unbranded cattle roamed Texas from the coastal plains in the south to the rolling hills and prairies in the north. Wild cattle were so plentiful that they had little value in Texas, but beef was in demand in the North and East where cattle herds had been depleted to feed the Union Army. A few enterprising and adventurous individuals began trailing their cattle to the nearest railroad where the cattle could be put on cars and shipped east.

Trail-driving pioneers such as Oliver Loving and Charles Goodnight drove herds of beef cattle to Army posts and Indian reservations in New Mexico and Arizona as early as 1866. The following year a cattle dealer named Joseph McCoy built a set of holding pens at Abilene, Kansas, and advertised that he would buy cattle from Texas. When the longhorn herds from Texas arrived in Kansas, McCoy shipped the cattle east over the railroad to the great meatpacking centers in Chicago. This secured a reliable

Charles Goodnight

One of the most successful ranchers on the Texas frontier, Charles Goodnight came to Texas as a child with his family in 1845, settling in Milam County. By the time he was twenty, he was running a herd of four hundred cattle in the Brazos River valley and soon established a ranch in Palo Pinto County in North Central Texas.

After service in the Civil War, Goodnight returned to his ranching interests in Palo Pinto County, and in 1866 he teamed up with veteran cattle raiser and trail driver Oliver Loving. The two men put together a herd of about two thousand head and drove them west where they sold the cattle to the Army at Fort Sumner, New Mexico, in order to feed Indians on the reservation. The trail blazed by the two cattle-driving pioneers went down in history as the Goodnight-Loving Trail, and over the next two decades tens of thousands of Texas longhorns went up the Goodnight-Loving to New Mexico, Colorado, and Wyoming.

In 1877 Goodnight formed a partnership with John Adair, a wealthy Englishman wanting to go into the cattle business. With Adair's money, Goodnight bought land in the Palo Duro Canyon area of the Texas Panhandle and established the famous JA Ranch. From this ranch Goodnight continued driving cattle north to Dodge City, Kansas, while reinvesting the profits in the ranch. By the time of Adair's death in 1885, Goodnight had increased the size of the JA to well over one million acres.

In addition to being one of Texas' most productive ranchers, Goodnight was civic minded and sought to improve the agricultural industry in Texas. He introduced Hereford bulls to the Panhandle to improve his herds and was the first Panhandle rancher to use barbed wire. He established a herd of buffalo on his ranch, possibly saving the animal from extinction, and introduced wheat farming to North Texas. In 1898 he and his wife Molly Dyer Goodnight founded Goodnight College. Living to the age of ninety-three, Charles Goodnight became a living legend and the epitome of the Texas rancher.

outlet for the cheap Texas cattle, and the Texas ranching industry soared. Over the next twenty years, the sale of millions of Texas cattle helped to revive the state's impoverished economy.

Ranchers on the Texas frontier helped to open up vast areas of West Texas and North Central Texas to settlement, while contributing to the economic stability and advancement of the state. In the decades following the Civil War, the ranching industry brought huge sums of cash into Texas, helping to revive the state after the economically crippling war. Early ranchers built homes and raised families, contributed to the building of churches and schools, organized counties and towns, and in many ways shaped the society of a large portion of the state.

SUGGESTED READINGS

Clayton, Lawrence and Joan Halford Farmer, eds. *Tracks Along the Clear Fork*. Abilene: McWhiney Foundation Press, 2000.

Dobie, J. Frank. *The Longhorns*. 1941. Austin: University of Texas Press, 1980.

Douglas, C.L. *Cattle Kings of Texas*. 1939. Austin: State House Press, 1989.

Haley, J. Evetts. *Charles Goodnight: Cowman and Plainsman*. 1936. Norman: University of Oklahoma Press, 1995.

Rister, Carl Coke. *Fort Griffin on the Texas Frontier*. 1956. Norman: University of Oklahoma Press, 1986.

Rodenberger, Lou, ed. *31 by Lawrence Clayton*. Abilene: McWhiney Foundation Press, 2002.

TEXAS
MYTHS
AND
LEGENDS

Artwork by member-artists of the
Center for Contemporary Arts, Abilene, Texas

Kitty Benson
Tony Brown
Tom Dunn
Barbara Edwards
Russell Ellison
Esme Glenn
Mary Kay Huff
Ruth Jackson
Martha Kiel
Bernice Landrum
Linda Murray
Tootsie Nichols
Nic Noblique
Sharon Rathbun
Catherine Sandell
Millie Sayre
Ginger Womack Taylor
Patty Rae Wellborn

Photographs by Steve Butman

Staff: Richard Metzger, Kathy Morehead, Ellery Flynn, Connie Petross

Center for Contemporary Arts
220 Cypress Street
Abilene, Texas 79601
(325) 677-8389

THE BUFFALO SOLDIER   THE COMANCHE WOMAN

THE
BUFFALO HUNTER

THE
SALOON GAL

THE RANCHER

THE COWBOY

THE TEXAS RANGER

THE OUTLAW

THE FRONTIER WOMAN

THE SODBUSTER

THE WILDCATTER

THE RAILROADER

THE COWBOY

The cowboy is perhaps the most dominant icon in Texas history, the most immediately recognized representative of the state. The cowboy may also be the most misunderstood and most heavily mythologized figure of our past. Although there are still authentic working cowboys in Texas today, the age of the classical open-range cowboy lasted only from about 1865 until perhaps 1895, or from the end of the Civil War until the closing of the American Frontier. But he made an impression on the American consciousness all out of proportion to his actual numbers and his time under the hot Texas sun.

Cowboys of the Texas frontier were almost always young men, seldom far beyond their teens. These men, who spent long hours in the saddle, were known by various names: brush popper, vaquero, buckaroo, hand or cowhand, waddy, drover, and puncher or cow puncher. The majority of the cowboys in Texas were white, but perhaps a third were Hispanic or black.

The unique clothing of the cowboy was strictly functional. While his shirt, trousers, and suspenders might resemble those of a factory worker in the East, the remainder of his outfit instantly identified him as a cowboy. The high-heeled boots were designed to keep the rider's foot from slipping through the stirrup, as it was a far better fate to be thrown from a horse than to be dragged. The broad-brimmed hat shaded the eyes and the protected the face from the sun and rain, while the cowboy's leather chaps protected his legs from mesquite and cactus thorns. The jingling spurs a cowboy wore were not ornamental but helped him to control horses that didn't want to be ridden. The cowhand's lariat, from the Spanish "la riata," enabled him to catch and secure elusive cattle and horses.

Taking care of cattle, whether on a ranch in West Texas or trailing a herd of steers from Bandera to Wyoming, was hard physical labor, often under the most brutal and grueling conditions. Cowboys got up before daylight, ate a hearty breakfast of beef, beans, and biscuits, caught up their mounts, and were in the saddle before sunup. They performed their work in the open, exposed to the broiling sun in the summer and the numbing cold of the winter. A cowboy's job was often a lonely one, and it required the ability to endure much hardship. Cowboys in general were independent, hard, tough men who wouldn't put up with a moaner or anyone who felt sorry for himself.

The job of tending cattle included rounding up the herds to brand the calves, doctoring sick cattle, pulling cows out of bog holes, and moving herds from one pasture to another. Hands on a cattle spread also built and repaired fences and windmills, cut cactus and brush, and repaired barns and corrals. Protecting the cattle from predatory animals such as wolves and cougars, as well as safeguarding the herds from rustlers, further occupied the cowboys' days. During his spare time a top hand might ride and train broncs, or unbroken horses.

While many Texas cowboys spent their working years on ranches, others hired on as drovers and went up the trail with herds to Kansas, New Mexico, Wyoming, or the Dakotas. A trail-driving cowpuncher might join a herd in South Texas below San Antonio and end up at a Kansas railhead or in the Dakotas supplying beef to an Indian reservation. Along the way the young waddy would traverse prairies, streams, and

"80 John" Wallace

Daniel Webster Wallace was born and raised in the fertile farming country of South Texas near Victoria, but he had no desire to work on a farm pulling cotton as he had grown up seeing his father do. Like many another young man of his time, Wallace wanted to be a cowboy.

As a young teenager barely fifteen years old, Wallace left his home and pursued his dream by hiring on as a hand with a large cattle outfit in Victoria County. Only one thing separated Wallace from other young cowboys of the time. Wallace, a young black man, had been born into slavery in 1860.

Wallace's first job as a puncher consisted of trailing a herd from Victoria to the vicinity of Buffalo Gap, near the present city of Abilene, Texas. Thus armed with actual trail-driving experience, young Wallace looked for and found more permanent employment on a ranch near Lampasas.

Gaining skill as a rider and cow-handler, Wallace became an excellent roper and proved himself to be a loyal and trustworthy hand. Soon he was on the move again, hiring on with a herd trailing out to Scurry County near present Snyder.

In 1878 the seventeen year-old Wallace went to work for Clay Mann, a well-known and successful rancher near Colorado City. Wallace worked for Mann for more than a decade, during which time Wallace became known as "80 John" after the "80" brand of the Mann herd. Mann was more than simply an employer to 80 John. Paying part of his wages in cattle, Mann encouraged Wallace to buy land for his own ranch. He taught the black cowboy how to manage money, how to buy and sell cattle, and how to conduct business.

After the death of Clay Mann in 1888, 80 John took up ranching for himself, successfully weathering droughts and recessions while buying more land and earning the admiration and respect of contemporary, mostly white, ranchers. At the time of his death in 1939, 80 John Wallace, a black man who had been born into slavery, was one of the most successful and well respected ranchers in West Texas. An exceptional man, he fully and successfully made the transition from cowboy to cattleman.

sometimes swollen rivers, while fighting boredom, herd-cutters, wolves, and an occasional band of hostile Indians. While roaming bands of Comanches and Kiowas provided anxiety and excitement, the fact was that more cowboys were killed by lightning or drowning than by Indians.

Sooner or later, cowboys grew too old to endure the harsh life a horseback job demanded. Cowboys too old or broken up by injuries sought employment in towns and cities, leaving the difficult job of punching cows to younger men.

During their age of ascendancy, Texas cowboys protected and promoted the agricultural industry that has been the lifeblood of Texas. They contributed to the economic stability of the state, helped to pave the way for more permanent settlers, and often became farmers or merchants themselves after giving up the nomadic horseback life.

SUGGESTED READINGS

Abbott, E.C., and Helena Huntington Smith. *We Pointed Them North: Recollections of a Cowpuncher.* Norman: University of Oklahoma Press, 1955.

Adams, Andy. *The Log of a Cowboy: A Narrative of the Old Trail Days.* Lincoln: University of Nebraska Press, 1963.

Clayton, Lawrence and Joan Halford Farmer, eds. *Tracks Along the Clear Fork.* Abilene: McWhiney Foundation Press, 2000.

Massey, Sarah, ed. *Black Cowboys of Texas.* College Station: Texas A&M Press, 2000.

Rodenberger, Lou, ed. *31 by Lawrence Clayton.* Abilene: McWhiney Foundation Press, 2002.

THE OUTLAW

While the vast majority of the inhabitants of the Texas frontier were relatively honest, law-abiding, and hard-working men and women, there were always a few individuals who ignored the conventions of civilization and became outlaws. The lack of a structured society and few law enforcement officers may have encouraged lawlessness among those inclined in that direction. Many who dabbled in extra-legal affairs desired an easy way to make money. These included pickpockets, thieves, burglars, rustlers, and robbers of banks, trains, and stagecoaches. Others had violent, homicidal natures and succumbed to their impulses to kill their fellow men.

Some men seemed to accidentally become outlaws, such as Will Carver, a cowboy from Bandera. Working on a ranch in Sutton County, Carver turned mean after his wife died in childbirth. First operating a saloon and gambling hall, Will soon took up armed robbery and murder-for-hire.

Other men could not resist the temptation when in close proximity to the money of others. Sam Bass sold a herd of cattle belonging to his neighbors, but instead of returning the money to its owners, he gambled and wasted it away on high living. Unable to return home empty-handed, he turned to robbing stagecoaches and trains.

Then some outlaws were simply vicious, cold-blooded killers, such as the infamous Texas gunman John Wesley Hardin. Raised during the violence-prone Civil War and Reconstruction era, Hardin killed his first man when only fifteen years old. He became the most notorious killer in Texas before his life of crime ended.

One of the few traits the different classes of criminals had in common was an aversion to hard work. Not that life on the owl hoot trail was easy or glamorous—far from it. Once an outlaw had acquired any degree of notoriety, he had to be very careful about where he went and how he traveled. If the outlaw had a reward of any size posted for his capture, he lived with the constant anxiety of a hunted animal. He could not openly go into towns for fear of being recognized by law officers and had to spend most of his time hiding out in the countryside. Sneaking into town to buy or steal food and supplies was neither exciting nor romantic. But then the smarter criminals did not seek fame and did not openly operate on the wrong side of the law.

The line separating outlaws from lawmen was sometimes an indistinct one, and some men traversed on first one side of the line and then the other. Fort Worth City Marshal Jim Courtright turned to murder-for-hire and extortion. John King Fisher, the South Texas rustler and general badman, apparently reformed and became so respectable that he became a deputy sheriff and then acting sheriff. An efficient and well-liked officer, he died when caught in the crossfire of a shootout in a San Antonio saloon. John Selman was a deputy sheriff, then turned to stealing cattle. After being run out of Texas, Selman organized a criminal gang in New Mexico, then returned to Texas and became a constable and gambler in El Paso before ultimately dying in a shootout with a deputy United States Marshal.

Few outlaws on the Texas frontier lived to enjoy retirement or experience the life of a respected elder citizen. The majority of those who robbed and killed for their livelihoods died early and violent deaths. Sam Bass the train robber died in a shootout with Texas Rangers while trying to hold up a bank. Jim Courtright died at the hands of a gambler he was trying to shake down. One of the last train robbers in Texas, Ben Kilpatrick died when a conductor struck him in the head with an ice mallet. The mad-dog killer John Wesley Hardin died with a bullet in the back, killed by someone seeking to enhance his own reputation.

John Larn

Some people don't know which side of the law they want to be on. Others just seem to have a fondness for other people's cows. John Larn, a friendly, popular young man from Alabama, had both of those problems.

After running away from home as a young teenager, Larn traveled to Colorado, Kansas, and New Mexico before coming to the Clear Fork of the Brazos country on the Texas frontier. Settling near Fort Griffin, he went to work for the Joe Matthews Ranch, where he came to appreciate the potential for prosperity in raising cattle in the Clear Fork Country. He also came to appreciate the youngest daughter of his employer and married her two years later.

As a member of one of the most respected families on the frontier, Larn joined the local vigilante group and made war on area rustlers. His success and popularity with the vigilantes, and his family connections, helped Larn win election for sheriff of Shackelford County in 1876. No one, least of all his wife, could have imagined that Larn was one of the biggest rustlers in the country.

During the first few months of his term, Larn enjoyed the support of the people of his county, but then area ranchers, including his in-laws, began suspecting him of being one of the rustlers he was sworn to oppose. Having lost the confidence of his constituents, Larn resigned as sheriff in March 1877 after serving not quite a year of his term.

Larn continued his cattle thieving and was suspected of killing people to whom he owed money. His depredations on his neighbors finally became too much, and one of his victims swore out a warrant for his arrest. A sheriff's posse arrested him and placed him in the county jail at Albany. On the night of June 24, 1878, a group of armed and masked vigilantes forced their way into the jail and disarmed the guards. John Larn died in a hail of gunfire in his cell in the Shackelford County jail.

From the earliest days, outlaws took advantage of the vast area of Texas to evade the law, and some criminals even achieved a measure of popularity in some quarters. While lawlessness in Texas flourished for a time, the coming of civilization with towns, peace officers, courts, and upright citizens brought about the demise of most outlaw elements and ushered in an era of increased peace and security to the Texas frontier.

SUGGESTED READINGS

Bartholomew, Ed. *Kill or Be Killed: A Record of Violence in the Early Southwest.* Houston: Frontier Press of Texas, 1953.

DeArment, Robert K. *Bravo on the Brazos: John Larn of Fort Griffin, Texas.* Norman: University of Oklahoma Press, 2002.

Holden, Francis Mayhew. *Lambshead Before Interwoven: A Texas Range Chronicle, 1848-1878.* College Station: Texas A&M University Press, 1982.

McGrath, Roger. *Gunfighters, Highwaymen, and Vigilantes: Violence on the Frontier.* Berkeley :University of California Press, 1984.

Miller, Rick. *Sam Bass & Gang.* Austin: State House Press, 1999.

Rodenberger, Lou, ed. *31 by Lawrence Clayton*. Abilene: McWhiney Foundation Press, 2002.

THE TEXAS RANGER

The earliest Anglo pioneers in Texas often had to defend themselves against marauding bands of hostile Indians. These settlers appealed to the Mexican government for protection, and in 1822 the Mexican governor of Coahuila-Texas authorized Stephen F. Austin, leader of the Anglo immigrants in Texas, to organize a regiment of militia to safeguard the colonies. Austin then hired a group of men "to act as rangers for the common defense."

These first Rangers were strictly Indian fighters, serving for short periods of time to pursue and punish raiding Indian parties, after which the Ranger companies disbanded. This practice continued during the years of the Republic of Texas and early statehood, during which Rangers were temporary citizen-soldiers organized as needed to fight pillaging Indians or invading Mexicans.

During the Mexican War of 1846-48, Texas Rangers served as guides and scouts for the U.S. Army. Using heavy Colt revolvers, designed by Ranger Captain Sam Walker, the Rangers intimidated and often brutalized their Mexican foes. After the war the U.S. Army assumed the traditional Ranger role of frontier and border defense, and the Ranger force languished for several years.

The American Civil War and Reconstruction eras were low points in Ranger history. During the war most Rangers and healthy young men in general took up arms under the Confederate flag, leaving the protection of the frontier to those too young, too old, or unfit to serve in the Southern Army. With the defeat of the Confederacy and the occupation of the South by Federal troops, the U.S. Army again assumed the burden of frontier protection. Neither the federal government nor the state Reconstruction government wanted large bands of armed Texas Rangers roaming the state.

The Army and the Reconstruction State Police had limited success in protecting the frontier against Indians, defending the southern border against Mexican raiders, or keeping citizens in the interior safe from criminals and violence. In 1874 the Reconstruction ended in Texas, and Governor Richard Coke and the Texas Legislature brought back the Texas Rangers. The Legislature organized the new Ranger force in two distinct units: the Special Force and the Frontier Battalion.

The Special Force, under the command of Captain Lee McNelly, went to South Texas and patrolled the area between the Rio Grande and the Nueces River. The Nueces Strip, as the brush-covered region was known, had long been a haven for outlaws from both sides of the border. Governor Coke gave Captain McNelly explicit instructions to clear up the lawless territory, no matter what the job required. McNelly and his Rangers may have been heavy-handed at times, and may have killed more bandits than they arrested, but they made the Nueces Strip a far safer place. The McNelly Rangers pursued cattle rustlers, fought Mexican bandits raiding from south of the border, and disarmed and disbanded armed mobs and vigilante posses. The efforts of McNelly and his Rangers ended an era of lawlessness in South Texas.

Major John B. Jones commanded the Frontier Battalion of the Texas Rangers from 1874 until he became adjutant general of the state in 1879. The Frontier Battalion had as its mission the protection of the Texas frontier from Indians. Six companies of seventy-five men each made up the Battalion, and their camps extended along the far reaches of civilization. Organized as an Indian-fighting force, the

Frontier Battalion engaged fourteen Indian raiding parties during the first six months of the Battalion's existence. During the next six months the Rangers had only six fights with Indians, and after May of 1875 the Indian threat on the frontier of Texas was all but eliminated.

With the Indian threat diminished, the Frontier Battalion turned its attention to domestic lawlessness and made a distinct transition from a military force to a state police agency. Acting as a permanent organization of state peace officers, the Rangers

Major John B. Jones

Rising from private to major in the Confederate Army gave John B. Jones a breadth of experience essential to successfully commanding troops in the field. When the Texas Legislature created the Frontier Battalion of the Texas Rangers in 1874, Governor Richard Coke chose Jones as the commander of the new organization. Tasked with the protection of the Texas frontier and given the rank of major, John B. Jones immediately organized six companies of Rangers and sent them to various points along the outer edges of civilized Texas.

Jones was an ideal commander for the time and place. A stern disciplinarian, Jones demanded and received professional behavior on the part of his Rangers, earning the respect and admiration of the public and the U.S. Army, alongside of which the Rangers sometimes fought. His administrative skill and organization contributed to the success of the Rangers, whether taking to the field in pursuit of raiding Comanches or concentrating their forces in the interior of the state to quell domestic violence and criminal behavior.

After the final defeat of the Comanche and Kiowa warriors in 1875 ended a half-century of Indian warfare, Major Jones turned the attention of the Frontier Battalion to crime suppression within the state. Jones and his Rangers ended the Mason County War, arranged a truce in the Horrell-Higgins feud, and arrested numerous wanted criminals, while restoring the public's confidence in state law enforcement and setting an example of efficiency and fairness. Making the transition from Indian fighter to state peace officer, Jones became the first modern Ranger, and his legacy lives on today.

of the Frontier Battalion ended riots, quelled feuds, and pursued and captured such notorious outlaws as John Wesley Hardin and Sam Bass.

The Texas Rangers of the 1870s and 1880s helped pave the way for settlement of much of the state. The Rangers live on to this day, as the oldest state police force in the United States.

SUGGESTED READINGS

Clayton, Lawrence and Joan Halford Farmer, eds. *Tracks Along the Clear Fork.* Abilene: McWhiney Foundation Press, 2000.

Proctor, Ben. *Just One Riot: Episodes of Texas Rangers in the 20th Century.* Austin: Eakin Press, 1991.

Robinson, Charles M. *The Men Who Wear the Star: The Story of the Texas Rangers.* New York: Random House, 2000.

Rodenberger, Lou, ed. *31 by Lawrence Clayton.* Abilene: McWhiney Foundation Press, 2002.

Utley, Robert. *Lone Star Justice: The First Century of the Texas Rangers.* New York: Oxford University Press, 2001.

Webb, Walter Prescott. *The Texas Rangers.* Boston: Houghton Mifflin, 1935.

THE SODBUSTER

While Texas is generally considered a ranching state, farming has been and continues to be an important component of the agricultural industry of the state. When early colonizers such as Stephen F. Austin brought the first American settlers to Texas, they brought farmers, not ranchers.

After the conclusion of the Civil War, many farmers from East Texas as well as other areas of the United States began moving farther west, lured by the abundance of inexpensive land. In the late 1870s and 1880s, large tracts of land owned by the public schools and the railroads became available for sale, leading to a mass migration of farmers, also known as sodbusters or nesters, to the more unsettled areas of the state. By the late 1870s farmers had come to the Texas frontier, bringing with them wagons pulled by oxen or mules and filled with wives, children, and possessions.

The number of farmers moving to the frontier regions of the state increased after the Texas and Pacific Railroad came to the area. Railroads were vitally important to farmers on the Texas frontier, bringing settlers to newly developing areas, while also owning much of the land that the farmers purchased. Railroads provided reliable transportation, allowing farmers to sell their produce in markets far from the sparsely settled farmlands.

As farmers settled along the Texas frontier, many of them raised crops they could sell for cash—primarily cotton but also wheat and sorghum. The new farming families moving to the edge of civilization in Texas first established individual farms, then small rural communities, the central point of which was often a cotton gin. The frontier farmers and their families soon built schools and churches, lending a sense of permanence to the communities.

Farming, especially in the early years in the frontier areas of Texas, was a difficult and risky way to make a living. While pioneer farmers in West Texas generally arrived after the Indian menace had been removed, there were other problems with which to contend. The earliest settlers in the area had been ranchers, some of whom ran their cattle on the open range without owning any property. In the 1880s there were confrontations between farmers, who fenced their property to protect their crops, and ranchers, who were accustomed to free range on which to graze their cattle.

Another problem for Texas farmers was rain, or the lack of it. The periodic droughts that afflict West Texas dashed the hopes of many farmers, causing some to abandon their farms and way of life. An uncertain market also caused anxiety and problems for farmers; they often did not know if they would be able to sell their produce for a profit or even be able to pay their debts.

In the days before tractors, farming was hard, physical labor. A farmer preparing new ground for a crop first had to cut down and burn any brush or scrub growth on the property. Once he cleared the land, the farmer then had to break the virgin sod with a single steel plow, pulled behind a mule or horse. After breaking the sod and planting his crop, the farmer spent long days under the scorching summer sun in the field with a hoe, "chopping cotton," or more accurately, chopping the weeds that grew up around the young cotton plants. In the fall, if sufficient rain had fallen at the right times, the farmer pulled the cotton bolls from the plants and transported the cotton to the gin, where the seeds were removed and cotton buyers waited to purchase the crop.

In addition to tending the cash crop, the frontier farmer had cows to milk, hogs to slop, wood to cut for fuel, and numerous other time-consuming chores to fill his days. Farming has always been a time-consuming, labor-intensive, risky business, dependent upon an abundance of rain, a lack of hail and insects, and the vagaries of

John B. Clack

In 1873 a group of adventurous young men from Tarrant County decided to try their luck at buffalo hunting in West Texas. Loading their rifles, ammunition, and other supplies in a wagon, the party headed west and eventually arrived at the rough and tumble frontier community of Buffalo Gap, in Taylor County, some 150 miles west of Fort Worth.

During the winter of 1873-74, John B. Clack, one of the buffalo hunters, and his companions had their share of adventures. The novice hunters learned how to stalk, kill, and skin the buffaloes. The group had encounters with bears and Comanche Indians, and Clack narrowly escaped injury or death when caught afoot in a buffalo stampede.

In the spring of 1874 the group returned with a wagon load of buffalo hides to Tarrant County, where young Clack obtained a job teaching school. In time he courted and married, but he never forgot his adventures on the Texas frontier, the beauty of the country, and the potential for opportunities there. In 1880 John B. Clack, his bride Mary Hampton Clack, and his brother M.M. Clack emigrated west to "grow up with the country."

Staking his claim on a section of land along Lytle Creek, J.B. Clack built a log cabin and turned his efforts to farming. Noticing the lack of fruits and vegetables available in the area, Clack planted peach trees, watermelons, potatoes, and other vegetables. Then plowing up larger areas of the prairie sod, Clack began growing corn and other grains as food for his family and milk cows.

As the county continued to grow in population, and in its demand for foodstuffs, Clack and other area farmers grew sorghum and wheat before finally settling on cotton as a cash crop. By his early efforts at planting and growing in an area many people deemed "hostile to agriculture," pioneer farmer John B. Clack proved that farming was possible and profitable on the Texas frontier.

price fluctuations. But in good years, farmers could pay off their grocery bills, buy new clothes for the family, and have money left over to buy additional land or to put in the bank to tide them over the lean years.

While coming to the frontier of Texas later than buffalo hunters and ranchers, farmers made a lasting impression on the land. Farmers, with their families, came to settle permanently and improve the land on which they toiled. The many farming communities along the Texas frontier are a testament to the vision and hardiness of the early farmers of Texas.

SUGGESTED READINGS

Caffey, David L. *The Old Home Place: Farming on the West Texas Frontier.* Burnet, Texas: Eakin Press, 1981.

Duff, Katharyn, and Betty Kay Seibt. *Catclaw Country: An Informal History of Abilene in West Texas.* Burnet, Texas: Eakin Press, 1980.

Fairchild, Louis. *The Lonesome Plains.* College Station: Texas A&M University Press, 2002.

THE FRONTIER WOMAN

Historians have traditionally relegated women to a secondary role in the taming of the frontier, when women are mentioned at all. Any serious consideration of frontier settlement, however, will show that women were instrumental in the permanent occupation of the West. Single men might build farms or ranches, but single men cannot and did not build families, or communities, or societies. Pioneer women were absolutely essential in transforming the frontier from a howling wilderness into homes for themselves, their families, and their descendents.

Women of wealth and ease did not initially come to the West, nor did the very poor. The majority of the women who settled the Texas frontier came from what we would today consider the middle class. Many who came out West were accustomed to the rugged life of a farm family or had grown up with chores and responsibilities more typical in an earlier age. A few were blushing brides with no idea of what to expect, while others had picked up and moved several times and thus were veteran pioneers. Whatever their background, the women who made it to the frontier were strong and healthy, as the weak and sickly died along the way. Those making the journey were also courageous, because the timid stayed at home in the East.

The pioneers who traveled from the settled portions of America to the Western frontier typically traveled in a Conestoga wagon, with all the possessions of the family contained inside. During a journey of a few days to several weeks, wives and mothers learned the difficulties of cooking, cleaning, and caring for their families while on the trail. Women moving West had to learn how to make beds in a wagon or erect tents for sleeping quarters while the men took care of the stock. Some young brides from comfortable middle class families had to learn such rudiments as how to make coffee and bake bread. They had to overcome their initial revulsion and collect buffalo chips and cow chips to use for their cooking fires when no wood was available. They had to deal with the annoyance of smoke from cooking fires, preparing meals with inadequate utensils, often only a single iron skillet, or trying to cook in the rain. Keeping children clean and clothes washed with a limited supply of water were especially trying. These and other difficulties the frontier women met, and conquered, while on the emigrant trail.

Upon their arrival the early settlers built new homes of whatever material was available. Some families initially lived in dugouts, or cave-like dwellings carved in the side of a small hill, then roofed over. Others built log cabins from cedar or pecan trees and chinked the cracks with mud, which often fell out when it dried, leaving gaps between the logs. The more fortunate families built their cabins of stone. For the early settlers, cabin floors were most often dirt, and other occupants of the homes included scorpions, spiders, mice, and occasionally snakes. Oilcloth, not glass, covered the windows, and the frontier wife prepared meals over an open fireplace until her husband could buy and install a wood-burning stove. Furnishings in the home were sparse and often primitive.

Families in early Texas had to be self-sufficient and women had to fill whatever role the situation demanded of them. Pioneer women had to be nurses, doctors, and midwives. Early wives had to set broken limbs, bandage cuts and burns, and treat the occasional gunshot wound and the more frequent snake bite. In addition to the traditional responsibility of maintaining their households, women on the Texas frontier also shared farming and ranching duties with their men.

Elizabeth Ann Carter Clifton

Among the first residents of Young County in the early 1850s were Elizabeth Ann and Alexander Carter. Moving to Texas from Alabama, the young couple settled near the frontier post of Fort Belknap. There the Carters farmed, raised livestock, and operated a freighting business. As if that were not enough to keep her busy, Mrs. Carter also opened and managed a boarding house.

In common with many frontier women, the life of Elizabeth Ann Carter was full of hardship and heartbreak. In 1857 an unknown assailant murdered her husband. The following year she took as her second husband an Army officer, Lieutenant Owen A. Sprague, but he disappeared only eight months after their marriage. During the following years Elizabeth Ann Carter continued to operate her boarding house and manage her ranch. Then in 1862 she married for the third time—to Thomas FitzPatrick, a local cowhand. Their wedded bliss ended a year and a half later with his death.

The trials of the frontier widow only increased. On October 13, 1864, a mixed group of Indians led by Comanche chief Little Buffalo attacked Elizabeth's ranch in the Elm Creek Raid. Indians murdered her daughter and infant grandson, then abducted Elizabeth, her thirteen-year-old son, and two granddaughters. Shortly after the raid the Indians killed her son.

For the next twelve months Elizabeth remained the captive of a band of Kiowa Indians in northwestern Kansas. Then in November 1865, U.S. soldiers rescued the enslaved woman. Following her release Elizabeth FitzPatrick journeyed to Parker County, where in 1869 she married Isaiah Clifton. Along with her only surviving granddaughter and her husband's children, Elizabeth and Isaiah Clifton settled near Fort Griffin in Shackleford County.

Having lived a life of adversity and suffering, Elizabeth Ann Clifton died in 1882 at the age of fifty-seven. Her life serves as a testament to the endurance and strength of the frontier women of Texas.

Early Texan adventurer Noah Smithwick quoted a pioneer lady as saying Texas was "a heaven for men and dogs, but a hell for women and oxen." Added to the hard work and drudgery was a lack of social interchange. Women on the Texas frontier often went months without seeing another white woman. Early diarists such as Susan Reynolds Newcomb complained bitterly of the isolation and loneliness. Occasionally women made the time to get together for church services, quilting bees, or community picnics and dances. The interaction with other women made the harsh life more bearable.

Ultimately, women pioneers survived and prospered and imposed civilization on the Texas frontier. In the absence of churches and schools, women provided the religious foundation and upbringing for their children and insisted on the best possible educations for their sons and daughters. Women brought a calming, stabilizing influence to the West and ushered in the era of communities, schools, churches, and civic clubs.

SUGGESTED READINGS

Burnett, Georgellen K. *We Just Toughed It Out: Women in the Llano Estacado*. El Paso: Texas Western, 1990.

Butler, Anne M., and Ona Siporin. *Uncommon Common Women: Ordinary Lives of the West*. Logan: Utah State University Press, 1996.

Exley, Jo Ella, ed. *Texas Tears and Texas Sunshine: Voices of Frontier Women*. College Station: Texas A&M University Press, 1985.

Matthews, Sallie Reynolds. *Interwoven: A Pioneer Chronicle*. 1936. College Station: Texas A&M Press, 1982.

Myres, Sandra L. *Westering Women and the Frontier Experience: 1800-1915*. Albuquerque: University of New Mexico Press, 1982.

THE RAILROADER

Reliable transportation is a vital necessity for any civilization. Transportation, whether by road, river, or rail, was essential for the socialization and commerce of people in early Texas. But Texas, so rich in land, was poor in navigable rivers. Use of waterways for trade and travel was seasonal and sporadic at best. The road situation was almost as bad. The elected commissioners of each county in early Texas had the responsibility for building and maintaining roads within their counties, and in the cash-strapped frontier areas few commissioners wanted to vote the funds needed to build long-distance thoroughfares. Railroads, then, were the ideal method of transportation in Texas. But the railroads were slow in coming.

The first Texas railroads were short lines, connecting one city to another or connecting seaports to nearby market centers. The very first Texas railroad opened in 1853 and ran from the port of Harrisburg, now on the Houston ship channel, to Stafford, some twenty-nine miles to the southwest. By the time the Civil War began, Texas had fewer than five hundred miles of railroad, and those were centered in Houston or other sea or river ports. During the war, little thought was given to new railroad construction, and at the war's end none of the railroads in Texas connected with those in any other state.

In 1869 the first transcontinental railroad opened and ushered in an era of extensive railroad building. The Texas and Pacific Railway Company began constructing a line across the state in 1872, reaching Dallas on July 1, 1873. Due to financial problems and a nationwide economic depression, the railway did not reach Fort Worth for another three years. The railroad then suspended work until April 1880, at which time construction to the west began in earnest. The railroad had come at last to the Texas frontier.

The Texas and Pacific, running across Texas from the Louisiana border to El Paso, was not the only railway important to the Texas frontier. The Fort Worth and Denver City ran from the cow town of Fort Worth north and west across the panhandle to New Mexico, and then north to the capital city of Colorado. And the Missouri, Kansas, and Texas entered the state from Indian Territory, later Oklahoma, and eventually reached Denison, Fort Worth, Wichita Falls, and points south.

Well-organized and hard-working groups of men built the railways across the Texas frontier. At the top of the railroad hierarchy were the owners and promoters. These were the men with the financial and political connections to get things done. Next were the construction engineers, responsible for the routes and the actual construction. Then came the construction foremen, gang bosses, and the laborers who did the physical work of building the roads.

After the surveying parties determined where the track should go, graders used scrapers, drawn by teams of horses and mules, to prepare the roadbed for the tracks. Much of the finishing work had to be done with shovels and picks. Then gangs of laborers laid the wooden crossties, and other men placed the iron rails upon the ties. In the final process yet more men spiked the rails into place, fastening them securely to the wooden ties. This process went on mile after mile, day after day, month after month, until the men completed the road.

Once the construction gang accomplished their task, another team of men took over. This new team consisted of the men who worked on the trains. The railroad engineer operated the engine, while the fireman fed the engine and kept it full of fuel. The brakemen manually applied brakes on the various cars of the train when going

Morgan Jones

Many of the men who worked the hardest to make our country a better place were immigrants. One such newcomer to Texas, and America, was the railroad builder Morgan Jones. Born and raised in Wales, Morgan Jones was the oldest son of a farming family. As a young lad he learned the value and importance of hard work, and at the age of twenty he left the family farm to work for the Cambrian Railroad in Southern Wales. An auspicious career in railroading had begun. During these early years, Jones learned the basics of railroad construction, how to handle men, and how to conduct business.

After several years in railroad construction in Wales, Jones realized that his home country offered limited opportunities for growth and advancement for a young man who wanted to build roads. Across the Atlantic, however, the North American continent offered unlimited opportunities for railroad building. The new world beckoned.

When the Civil War ended in America in 1865, twenty-six year-old Morgan Jones immigrated to the United States. His experience building railroads impressed General Granville Dodge, chief engineer for the Union Pacific Railway Company, who hired the young Welshman as the foreman of a construction crew. The meeting of these two men was fortuitous for each of them and of great benefit to the railroad industry in general in the United States. During the next two years, Jones worked on the first transcontinental railroad and, after its completion, built sections of the Texas and Pacific Railroad. His experience in building those two lines established Jones as a reliable and respected builder of railroads.

In addition to the major lines, Morgan Jones also built numerous short-line railroads across north and west Texas, opening up those areas to farming and settlement. During a career that spanned more than forty years, Morgan Jones built a network of rail lines that tied the isolated communities of West Texas and North Texas together and linked them to a nationwide rail system. His service to his adopted state earned for Morgan Jones the title of "Greatest Railroad Builder in Texas."

down a grade. Finally, the conductor interacted with the traveling public and had overall control and authority of the train. Behind these men, of course, was a complete support staff that included ticket agents, baggage handlers, telegraph operators, and many others.

Railroads were of inestimable importance to the Texas frontier. Railroads opened up new areas to settlement, spurred the growth of towns, and tied farmers and ranchers to markets in other parts of the country. Railroads, and the men who built and operated them, made it possible to live and prosper on the Texas frontier.

SUGGESTED READINGS

Braudaway, Douglas. *Railroads of Western Texas*. Charleston: Arcadia Publishing, 2000.

Reed, S.G. *A History of the Texas Railroads*. Houston: St. Clair Publishing Co., 1941.

Spence, Vernon Gladden. *Colonel Morgan Jones: Grand Old Man of Texas Railroading*. Norman: University of Oklahoma Press, 1971.

Zlatkovich, Charles P. *Texas Railroads: A Record of Construction and Abandonment*. Austin: University of Texas Press, 1981.

THE WILDCATTER

By the middle of the twentieth century, oil and the wealth it produced had become almost synonymous with Texas. When people from other states or other countries think of Texas, images of cowboys and oil wells often come to mind. But Texas was not always a land of oil, and, ironically, in the early days water-starved Texans considered oil more of a curse than a blessing.

Early Texas settlers digging wells for water found the first oil in our state. Men needing water for their own consumption, as well as for their livestock and crops, were bitterly disappointed when they found the thick, black liquid. The first oil discovery in West Texas occurred in 1878 in Brown County when Martin Meinsinger, seeking water, found oil at a depth of only 102 feet. Making the best of a bad situation, the enterprising well-digger bottled the sticky substance and sold it as a medicine and as a lubricant for squeaky wheels.

Prior to the advent of the internal combustion engine, the dominant product made from oil was kerosene for lamps, and the limited demand for kerosene kept the price of oil low. As automobiles became more popular, demand for gasoline, and the oil from which it was made, grew enormously. By the early years of the twentieth century, oil exploration in Texas had begun. Beginning in East Texas, oil exploration and production soon moved west. The first successful well drilled for the purpose of finding oil in the newly settled, western region of the state was in 1910 in Coleman County, where oil was found at a depth of four hundred feet.

Many of the most successful oil discoveries in Texas were "wildcat" ventures, or wells drilled in unproven territory, in search of new fields. A wildcatter is a driller or producer who is willing to take a chance on the unknown, on the unproven, hoping to find oil where the big companies disdain to seek it. So the wildcatter is a gambler, a risk-taker, and fit in well with the popular concept of the Texas frontier.

In the 1870s buffalo and Comanche Indians inhabited North-central Texas, the area between Fort Worth and Abilene. By the end of the nineteenth century farmers and ranchers had replaced the Indians, and cattle replaced the buffalo. In the early years of the twentieth century, a new breed of pioneers moved into the region, as oil production became the dominant force in that area. After the first gusher blew in at the Eastland County town of Ranger in October 1917, an invading army of lease hounds, geologists, landmen, drillers, and roughnecks descended on the area. As gusher after gusher erupted, the population of Ranger exploded from less than one thousand to more than thirty thousand people within a few short months.

After the initial discovery in Ranger, additional discoveries followed quickly in Desdemona, in Eastland County; Breckenridge, in Stephens County; then Burkburnett and Electra, in Wichita County. The output of these fields amounted to millions of barrels of oil per year, although some of the fields played out quickly. These oil discoveries came during the trying days of World War I, when oil shortages hampered the war effort. As a result of the oil produced by the Ranger Field, the British prime minister declared that the Allies "floated to victory on a wave of oil."

As the discovery fields began to play out, oil production moved further west, leading to enormous discoveries in the Permian Basin region of West Texas. One of the most famous wells in that area is the Santa Rita Number 1 in Reagan County, a well drilled on University of Texas land and named for the saint of the impossible.

Blowing in on May 28, 1923, Santa Rita Number 1 proved the potential of the

Permian Basin and added enormous wealth to the coffers of state universities.

From the earliest days, oil money has helped local institutions, hospitals, colleges,

and numerous worthy causes. Oil wealth contributed immeasurably to the benefit of Texas

and Texans, and the economic impact of oil to the fading frontier was enormous.

William Knox Gordon

In 1917 Eastland County, like much of Texas, was in the midst of a severe drought that had lasted for years. Crops failed, grasslands withered, and the value of livestock plummeted. In this desperate economic situation, citizens from the small West Texas community of Ranger pleaded with W. K. Gordon to see if he could find oil in the surrounding region. Gordon, a vice president of the Texas and Pacific Coal Company, was a well-known and well-respected figure in the area, a man to be relied upon in desperate times.

Born and raised in Virginia, William Knox Gordon learned geology and engineering from an uncle before beginning a career surveying for railroads in Virginia and throughout the South. He came to Texas in 1889 to survey a rail route and ended up taking a job as a mining engineer for the Texas and Pacific Coal Company in Thurber, Texas. Moving up quickly, Gordon became a vice president in the company and

manager of the coal company, which included operation of the company-owned town of Thurber.

While searching for new coalfields, Gordon became convinced that oil lay beneath the surface of the land north and west of Thurber. Despite reports from geologists saying there was no oil in the area, Gordon began buying up oil leases on behalf of his company. Spurred on by the entreaties of desperate farmers, Gordon gambled on his instincts and, in a wildcat venture, drilled on the McCleskey farm near Ranger. On a cool Saturday afternoon in October 1917, the well came in and started flowing. Black gold had come to Ranger, Texas.

The discovery of huge oil deposits in the vast Ranger Field not only alleviated the plight of area landowners but also eased the critical oil shortage that adversely impacted the defense efforts of our nation during World War I.

SUGGESTED READINGS

House, Boyce. *Were You in Ranger?* Dallas: Tardy, 1935.

Olien, Roger M. and Diana Davids Olien. *Oil in Texas: The Gusher Age, 1895-1945*. Austin: University of Texas Press, 2002.

Rister, Carl Coke. *Oil!: Titan of the Southwest*. Norman: University of Oklahoma Press, 1949.

Woodward, Don. *Black Diamonds! Black Gold!: The Saga of Texas Pacific Coal and Oil Company*. Lubbock: Texas Tech University Press, 1998.

John C. Ferguson grew up in Cisco in North Central Texas, an area that a century before had been the frontier of Texas. He was the restoration planner at the Battleship *Texas* State Historic Site near Houston before becoming director of the 12th Armored Division Museum in Abilene. He also teaches history at Cisco Junior College.